Chapter One:

The Little Lion

The boys were on the football pitch waiting for the match to start. They practised dribbling, running and taking shots on goal. Their coach paced the touchline, looking anxiously at his watch. He went across to Rodrigo, the team captain, who was talking to an old lady. There was a small boy in a football kit standing next to them.

"Hey, Rodrigo! We're a player short," the coach said, crossly.

Rodrigo pointed to the little boy.

"He can play for us," he said.

The coach laughed and shook his head.

"Are you joking? He's too young, and far too small. There are some big lads out there. He'd get knocked over as soon as he touched the ball!"

"Nonsense!" snorted the old lady, looking in the direction of the opposition team. "He'll run rings round that load of lumbering elephants. He's a little magician with the ball." She turned to the older boy. "Isn't he, Rodrigo?"

Rodrigo nodded. "This is my grandmother," he explained to the coach. He turned to the small boy. "And this is my kid brother."

The coach sighed. The little lad was half the size of the other players, but he supposed that having ten-and-a-half players in his team was better than having just ten.

"So, you want to play football with us?" he asked the small boy.

The boy nodded, too shy to speak.

"Tell you what," said the coach. "You play here on the wing." He turned to the grandmother and whispered: "Then if he gets knocked over and starts to cry, you can grab hold of him and take him home."

The first time the little boy got the ball he didn't know what to do with it. It just bounced away. The next time he got the ball, he dribbled it down the pitch.

"Pass it!" yelled the coach.

But the small boy kept running with the ball. He skipped over one player, then another and another. The coach stared at him in awe.

"I told you he was a magician with the ball," said the grandmother, proudly.

"You're right," replied the coach. "What did you say his name was?"

"Lionel," replied the grandmother. "It means 'little lion'."

Chapter Two:

Devastating News

Word quickly got round about the amazing ability of the "little lion". Soon Lionel Messi was playing in the boys' football team run by Newell's Old Boys

Athletic Club, the oldest, largest and most famous football club in Rosario, the town in Argentina where he lived.

Wherever Lionel played, people didn't stop talking about him.

"Such skill! In such a young boy! It's a shame he's such a small lad."

"Oh, don't you worry. He'll grow. They all do."

But Lionel didn't grow. The other boys his age started to get taller and stronger. Lionel stayed the same size.

Eventually, when he was nine, his mother and father took him to see a specialist doctor at the hospital. The doctor did all sorts of tests. A few weeks later, he called the family back into the hospital to discuss the results.

"Lionel is a very healthy boy," he explained. "But he does have a growth-hormone deficiency."

"What does that mean?" asked Lionel's mum.

The doctor shrugged. "Just that he'll always be very short."

"Too short to become a professional footballer?" asked Lionel's dad.

The doctor nodded. "Certainly, there will be no way he could make it to the top."

Lionel's heart sank at the devastating news. He stared at the floor. He didn't dare look up in case the doctor and his mum and dad saw his tears.

"Of course, if he were to take a daily course of hormone injections, there is every chance that he would start to grow properly again. But I should warn you that treatment is very expensive. And he would need to take the treatment for six years — until he is sixteen."

Lionel stayed staring at the floor. Expensive medical treatment was something his parents could not afford, he knew. His dad worked in a steel factory and his mum was a part-time cleaner. They already struggled to make ends meet.

Lionel's father stood up. "Celia," he said to Lionel's mum, "take the boy home. I will see you back there this evening."

"Where are you going, Jorge?" Lionel's mum asked.

But Lionel's dad walked out of the hospital without a word.

That evening, while he slumped on the sofa watching TV, Lionel heard his dad come in. He heard him talking to his mum in the kitchen. After a while, they came through and sat down with Lionel.

"Lionel," his dad said to him, "I've been down to Newell's Old Boys."

"What for?" asked Lionel. "To tell them I'll never be tall enough to become a professional footballer?"

Lionel's dad shook his head and smiled. "I told them what the doctor said. They are so confident of your footballing talent, they've offered to help pay for your course of treatment!"

Chapter Three:

The Machine of '87

Every night before going to sleep, Lionel had to give himself his hormone injection. It really hurt and he didn't like doing it, but he knew it was the only way he would get to grow to a height where he could realise his dream of playing professional football.

Before each match, Lionel and the other boys in the team would practise their skills on the pitch. Lionel liked to do keepy-uppies: keeping the ball in the air using just your feet and knees. Lionel's keepy-uppies began to become quite famous with the local people who had turned up to watch the game.

One day, a man in the crowd shouted out, "Hey, Lionel, do us a hundred keepy-uppies and these are yours!" He held out a handful of coins.

The other people in the crowd laughed, but Lionel quietly grabbed a ball, placed it at his feet and kicked it into the air. He knocked it back up again with his knee and then his foot. Soon, everyone was watching him. He reached a hundred keepy-uppies, then kicked

the ball hard and high skywards. The
people on the touchline cheered. The
man who had issued the challenge to
Lionel shouted "Bravo!" and threw him
a handful of coins.

Lionel's keepy-uppies became a regular feature of the team's pre-match warm ups. His record was 1,200 touches! Each time he completed a keepy-uppy challenge, people would throw coins to him. It was a good way to make some money.

Lionel was indeed a "magician" with the ball, but the Newell's Old Boys junior team he played in was full of high-quality players. In four years, the team only lost one match! They became nicknamed "The Machine of '87", because, like Lionel, all the boys playing had been born in 1987.

With his daily hormone-growth treatment and his regular training and playing in a talented team of young footballers, Lionel continued to grow, both in height and as a footballer. Three years after he had begun his treatment, he was ready for the next step towards his dream of becoming a top professional. He was thirteen. He and his team-mates would soon be moving up to the under-sixteen's team. It was an exciting time.

Later that year, Lionel began to notice that his mum and dad seemed to have even less money than usual. They weren't able to afford the new football boots he'd been hoping for at Christmas.

"Sorry, son," said his dad. "We're short of money. It's the economic crisis."

Lionel had heard about the "economic crisis" on the TV news. He knew that many people were out of work, and even those with jobs were struggling for money.

One day, Lionel and his parents were called in for a meeting with the Newell's Old Boys Director of Football. His face was grim.

"Times are tough, as you know," he said with a sigh, "and the club is short of money. I'm afraid we won't be able to contribute to the cost of Lionel's medical treatment any longer."

Lionel sat, stony-faced. He knew his parents wouldn't be able to pay for his growth-hormone treatment without the club's help.

And without that treatment, he would never be tall or strong enough to play professional football.

Suddenly, all the dreams, the hopes and the plans he had for the future seemed to have been smashed.

Chapter Four:
Barcelona

Now that a career as a top football professional was out of the question, Lionel began to wonder what the future might hold for him.

Art was his favourite subject at school.

Deep down though, he guessed that once he left school, he would end up working at the steel factory alongside his father.

One evening, Lionel came home from football training to find his mum waiting for him in the hall.

"Get yourself smartened up," she hissed. "Put a clean shirt on and for goodness' sake do try and drag a comb through your hair. There's someone here to see you."

Lionel got changed, then went through to the front room where a man in a grey suit was sitting on the sofa. Lionel's dad sat opposite him, perched on the edge of a chair. There was an expression on his face that Lionel couldn't quite make out. His dad seemed to be both excited and nervous at the same time.

"This gentleman is a football club scout," Lionel's dad said.

The scout shook Lionel's hand. "I keep an eye on some of the youngsters coming through the junior teams in Rosario. Your keepy-uppies are very famous in the city here!" He smiled. "When I spoke to Newell's Old Boys, they told me all about your need for medical treatment. I've been in touch with a professional club who will be happy to meet all your medical expenses."

Lionel frowned. He knew that all the other professional clubs in Argentina were short of cash, just like Newell's Old Boys.

Lionel's dad looked serious. "The thing is, son, it's not an Argentinian club. It's a European one. Barcelona."

Lionel gasped. He had never been away from home before; never left South America. But Barcelona! Newell's Old Boys might be one of the biggest clubs in South America, but Barcelona was one of the biggest clubs in the world.

"Well, son," Lionel's dad said, quietly. "Barcelona's a long way away. It's a big club. It's a big chance. It's a big decision — a decision only you can make."

Chapter Five:

The Contract

Lionel's dream was to play professional football. But he was worried. Supposing Barcelona didn't think he was good enough? He was only thirteen, after all. He wished his gran was around to give him some encouragement, like she had done when he was little, but she had died a couple of years before. Lionel still missed her. But she would've encouraged him to go, he knew.

And so, a few months after the football scout's visit, Lionel and his dad boarded a flight to Spain.

Lionel was to have a week's trial, training and playing with the different Barcelona youth squads. He and his dad stayed in a hotel close to the Nou Camp, Barcelona's football ground.

The man who would decide whether or not Lionel would be offered a contract was the club's technical director, Charly Rexach. He was away watching the Sydney Olympic Games until the end of the week. While they waited, Lionel's dad hired an agent to help Lionel secure a good deal.

On the last day of his trial, Lionel was put into one of the youth teams for a proper match. Charly Rexach had got back from Australia the night before and was sitting in the dugout.

Just seven minutes into the game, Charly Rexach turned to his youth team coach and said: "OK, he's small, but look at that confidence, look at his speed! See the way he dodges round defenders without any hesitation at all! We have to sign him! Now!"

But although Charly Rexach might have been keen to buy Lionel, the rest of the directors at Barcelona weren't so sure.

"He's small," they complained. "And he needs medical treatment, which we will have to pay for!"

One week turned into two, and still there was no decision. While the

Barcelona board argued about whether to buy him or not, Lionel quietly went about training with the youth teams. His dad spent his days pacing the touchline or moping about the hotel. When were Barcelona going to make a decision?

With Christmas approaching, Lionel's dad's patience finally snapped.

"They can't keep the boy waiting for an answer any longer!" he told Lionel's agent. "Do they want him or not?"

Lionel's agent met Charly Rexach in a restaurant.

"We need an answer. If we don't get one, the boy and his father are leaving."

"Where will you go? Back to Newell's Old Boys?"

The agent shook his head. "We'll go to Real Madrid!"

Real Madrid were — and still are — Barcelona's biggest rivals.

Without another word, Charly Rexach took his pen from his pocket and grabbed the nearest piece of paper he could find: a serviette that was tucked neatly into his wine glass. On the serviette he wrote a short contract and signed it.

Soon after, Lionel received his official club ID card.

FEDERACIÓ CATALANA
DE FUTBOL

- 6 MARÇ 2001

RADA: 2000-2001

EL ANDRES
I

Chapter Six:
The Decision

The following February the rest of Lionel's family — his mum, two brothers and little sister — joined him and his dad in Barcelona. Lionel was happy. He had his family with him and he was now a student at Barcelona football club's famous youth academy, "La Masia". He was playing football every day.

By the summer though, things weren't looking so good. Lionel's mum, brothers and little sister had not settled in Barcelona and were very unhappy.

Lionel's dad called the family together to discuss things.

"There's only one question really," said Lionel's dad. "Do we stay or do we go?"

"I want to go back to Argentina!" yelled Lionel's little sister.

Lionel's brothers nodded in agreement.

"I shall go home with them then," said Lionel's mum, softly.

All eyes turned to Lionel.

"If you decide to call it a day with Barcelona, we'll all go back to Argentina together," said his father. "If you decide to stay, I'll stay in Barcelona with you." He paused. "So, son, what's it to be?"

Lionel looked round at his family. What did he want to do? He thought that deciding whether or not to come to Barcelona had been hard enough, but this was even harder! Staying would split up his family. Going back home to Argentina would mean giving up his dream.

Chapter Seven:

Goal!!!!!!!

Lionel took a deep breath. "I'll stay," he whispered. His mum started to cry and he felt his eyes begin to prickle. For a moment, he almost changed his mind.

"I'll see you all during the summer holidays and at Christmas and Easter," said Lionel. He thought about his gran: the one member of his family he wouldn't be seeing again. He knew she would've wanted him to stay at Barcelona.

Over the next four years, time flew by for Lionel Messi. He continued to grow in height and strength, making a name for himself in the youth and reserve teams.

As time went on, Lionel began to wonder if he'd ever make it into the first team. But then a new coach, Frank Rijkaard, arrived and put the 17-year-old into the squad for a league match. He came on as a substitute, but he didn't do much and nobody really noticed him. Barcelona fans were used to young kids coming through to the first team from the junior squads.

A few months later, Lionel came on again as a substitute six minutes from time in a league match against Albacete.

He'd only been on a minute when he got a superb through ball from his team-mate, the Brazilian star Ronaldinho.

Keeping the defenders at bay, he dinked the ball over the Albacete keeper's head.

It was a brilliant goal. He turned round to celebrate with his team-mates. But they were standing around with frustrated looks, their hands on their hips. Out of the corner of his eye Lionel saw the linesman's flag was

up. Lionel's first goal for Barcelona had been ruled offside!

Ronaldinho came over and gave Lionel an encouraging pat on the back. "That linesman needs glasses," he said. "Don't worry, you've scored once, you can score again. There's another five minutes left till full-time."

But Albacete were intent on closing the match down. They packed players into their box. There was no way through for Lionel. He glanced up at the scoreboard clock: only two minutes to the final whistle.

He saw the ball was with Ronaldinho again. Ronaldinho fed a pinpoint pass through to Lionel, just like the one he'd made before. Lionel collected the ball and once again, dinked it over the keeper.

"Goal!!!!" roared the crowd. And this time there was no offside flag. The players and the fans went wild. They had just witnessed a fantastic goal from a youngster who they knew would become a club legend.

Lionel looked up to the sky, just like he does for every goal he scores for Barcelona. It's his way of saying thank you to his grandmother, who first encouraged him to follow his dream of becoming a footballer all those years ago.

Fact file
Leo Messi

Full name: Lionel Andrés Messi

Born: 24 June 1987,
Rosario, Argentina

Height: 1.70 metres

Honours

— 2009
Ballon d'Or ["Golden Ball"] Award for the European
Footballer of the Year and FIFA World Player of the Year

— 2010
FIFA Ballon d'Or ["Golden Ball"] Award for the Best
Footballer in the World

— 2011
FIFA Ballon d'Or and UEFA Best Player in Europe Award

— 2012
FIFA Ballon d'Or

— 2015
UEFA Best Player in Europe Award

Records

— Most Ballons d'Or (4 between 2009 and 2012)

— La Liga top goal scorer: 2009—2010, 2011—2012, 2012—2013

— Top goal scorer in La Liga: 289 goals

— Top goal scorer in UEFA Champions League: 77 goals

— Top goal scorer in all club competitions in a season:
73 goals in 2011—12

— Top goal scorer for club and country in a calendar year:
91 goals in 2012

— Only player to score at least 40 goals in 6 consecutive
seasons in La Liga: from 2009—2010 to 2014—2015

The Leo Messi Foundation

The Leo Messi Foundation supports access to health care,
education and sport for children in Spain, Argentina and
other countries.

Louis Smith

"So, you've brought Louis to be auditioned for the cathedral choir?" asked the man behind the piano. He could see Louis fidgeting and looking bored. "Well, I suppose I'd better hear him sing."

So Louis sang.

When he had finished, Louis' mum turned to the man behind the piano and said, "What do you think, then?"

The man slowly smiled. "I think Louis has a most wonderful voice. I'd be delighted to offer him a place in the cathedral choir."

Continue reading this story in:
DREAM TO WIN:
Louis Smith